# Dino-sitting

Written and illustrated by Steve Smallman

Nutter loved to hit things with his head.

He hit trees...

and he hit rocks.

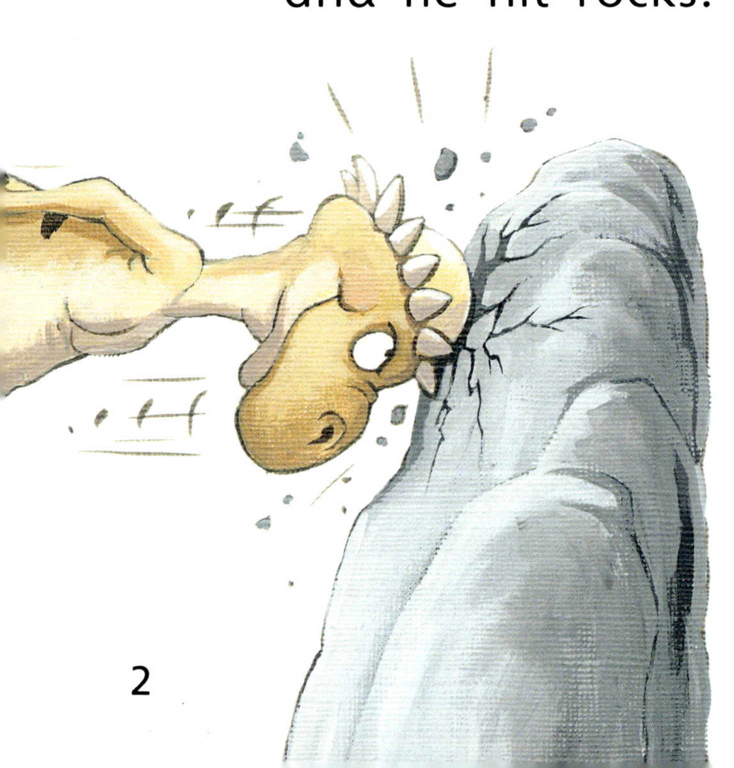

"Crash!" he shouted, as an old tree fell to the ground.

Nutter sat down. He was happy and dizzy. Then he saw something on the ground under some leaves. It was an egg.

"Oh no!" said Nutter. "It must have fallen out of a nest in the tree!"

Nutter looked in the tree for a nest.
He could not find one.

He held the egg up to his ear.

Something was inside it!

Nutter didn't know what to do, so he ran off to get help.

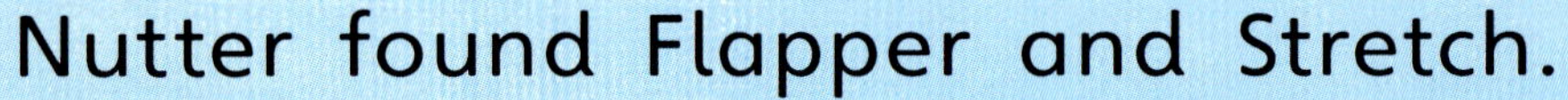

Nutter found Flapper and Stretch.
"Look at this egg," he said.
"How did you get it?" asked Stretch.

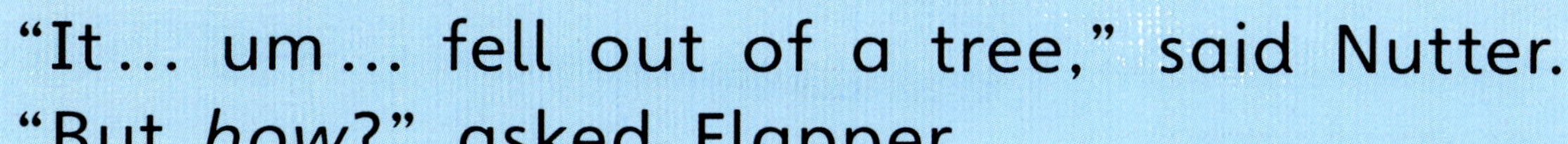

"It… um… fell out of a tree," said Nutter.

"But *how*?" asked Flapper.

"I hit the tree with my head," said Nutter.

"Oh, Nutter!" cried Flapper. "We must make a new nest for it."

Stretch and Nutter made a nest from some leaves.

Flapper gently put the egg into the nest.

“The egg feels a bit cold,” said Stretch.

“What can we do?” asked Nutter.

“Somebody will have to sit on the egg to keep it warm,” said Flapper.

"Who?" asked Nutter.
"YOU!" cried Flapper and Stretch.

Nutter sat down carefully on the egg.

He waited,

and waited,

and waited.

CRACK!

The egg broke open and something came out... but it wasn't a bird.

“What is it?” asked Nutter.

“I don’t know,” said Flapper. “But it looks hungry!”

It didn't want to eat a plant...

or a fish.

"So what does it eat?" asked Nutter.

Ouch!

"I think it wants to eat US!" said Stretch.

"Oh no!" cried Flapper. "It's a baby T-rex!"

Stretch and Flapper got the baby T-rex to let go of Nutter's bottom.

Then they took it back to where Nutter had found the egg... but something else was there, too.

ROOOAAR!

A huge T-rex was looking in the bushes. Nutter quickly put the baby T-rex down on the ground next to a tree.

"Now there's only one thing left to do," whispered Nutter.

"What?" said Stretch.

# "RUN!"